W9-AON-952

020
MIL

Miller, Heather
Librarian

$21.36
BC#34880000025663

DATE DUE	BORROWER'S NAME	

020
MIL

BC#34880000025663 $21.36

Miller, Heather
Librarian

Morrill E.S.
Chicago Public Schools
1431 North Leamington Avenue
Chicago, IL 60651

This Is What I Want to Be

Librarian

Heather Miller

Heinemann Library
Chicago, Illinois

©2003 Reed Educational & Professional Publishing
Published by Heinemann Library,
an imprint of Reed Educational & Professional Publishing
Chicago, IL

Customer Service 888-454-2279
Visit our website at www.heinemannlibrary.com

Designed by Sue Emerson, Heinemann Library
Printed and bound in the United States by Lake Book Manufacturing, Inc.

07
10 9 8 7 6 5 4 3 2

Library of Congress Cataloging-in-Publication Data
Miller, Heather.
    Librarian / Heather Miller.
       p. cm. — (This is what I want to be)
Includes index.
Contents: What do librarians do?—What is a librarian's day like?—What tools do librarians use?—Where do librarians work?—What do school librarians do?—When do librarian work?—Do librarians work in other places?—What kinds of librarians are there?—Quiz.
   ISBN: 978-1-4034-0369-8 (1-4034-0369-4) (HC), ISBN 978-1-4034-0591-3 (1-4034-0591-3) (Pbk)
   1. Librarians—Juvenile literature. 2. Library science—Vocational guidance—Juvenile literature.
   3. Librarians—Juvenile literature. [1. Librarians. 2.Libraries. Occupations.] I. Title. II. Series
Z682 .M55 2002
020'.92—dc21

                              2001008607

Acknowledgments
The author and publishers are grateful to the following for permission to reproduce copyright material:

p. 4 Michael Newman/PhotoEdit; p. 5 Flash! Light/Stock Boston; p. 6 Richard Hutchings/Corbis; p. 6 Terry Allen/ International Stock; p. 7 Jon Riley/Stone/Getty Images; p. 8 Cassy Cohen/PhotoEdit; p. 9 3M; p. 10 Rafael Macia/Photo Researchers, Inc.; pp. 11, 18L Mug Shots/Corbis Stock Market; p. 12 Guy Cali/Stock Connection/PictureQuest; pp. 13, 21 Brian Warling/Heinemann Library; p. 14 Jeff Isaac Greenberg/Photo Researchers, Inc.; p. 15 PhotoLink/PhotoDisc; p. 16 Michael Paras/International Stock; p. 17 Bob Daemmrich/Stock Boston; p. 18R Heinemann Library; p. 19 George Ancona/ Photo Researchers, Inc.; p. 20 Jose Luis Pelaez Inc./Corbis Stock Market; p. 23 (row 1, L-R) Jeff Isaac Greenberg/Photo Researchers, Inc., Heinemann Library; p. 23 (row 2, L-R) PhotoLink/PhotoDisc, Cassy Cohen/PhotoEdit; p. 23 (row 3) Jon Riley/Stone/Getty Images

Cover photograph by EyeWire Collection
Photo research by Scott Braut

Every effort has been made to contact copyright holders of any material reproduced in this book. Any omissions will be rectified in subsequent printings if notice is given to the publisher.

Special thanks to our advisory panel for their help in the preparation of this book:

Eileen Day, Preschool Teacher
Chicago, IL

Ellen Dolmetsch, MLS
Wilmington, DE

Kathleen Gilbert,
Second Grade Teacher
Austin, TX

Sandra Gilbert,
Library Media Specialist
Houston, TX

Angela Leeper,
Educational Consultant
North Carolina Department
of Public Instruction
Raleigh, NC

Pam McDonald, Reading Teacher
Winter Springs, FL

Melinda Murphy,
Library Media Specialist
Houston, TX

Special thanks to the faculty and students at Stockton School, Chicago, Illinois, for their help in the preparation of this book.

Some words are shown in bold, **like this.**
You can find them in the picture glossary on page 23.

Contents

What Do Librarians Do?

Librarians help people find answers.

They help people find books at the library.

Librarians teach people how to use **computers.**

What Is a Librarian's Day Like?

Librarians put special numbers and letters on new books.

The numbers and letters help people find the books they need.

Librarians read about new books.

They choose new books for
the library.

What Tools Do Librarians Use?

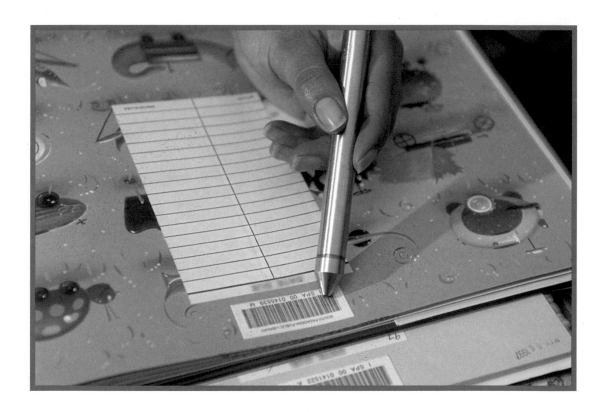

Librarians use **scanning wands**.

These tell the **computer** when books are checked out.

These special gates make loud sounds.

They tell librarians which books
have not been checked out.

Where Do Librarians Work?

Some librarians work in public libraries.

Many people visit the library to borrow books.

Other librarians work in school libraries.

School libraries lend books to students and teachers.

What Do School Librarians Do?

School librarians teach children.

They help children learn how to find things in books.

School librarians often work
with teachers.

They make sure teachers have the
books they need.

Do Librarians Work in Other Places?

Some librarians drive **bookmobiles.**

They bring books to people who do not live near a library.

Some librarians work with
businesspeople.

They help businesspeople find
the facts they need.

When Do Librarians Work?

Most librarians work during the day.

But some libraries are open late at night.

School librarians work on
school days.

They get the library ready
before school begins.

What Kinds of Librarians Are There?

Reference librarians help people find facts.

They help people use **reference books**.

Children's librarians work with young readers.

They tell stories and sing songs.

How Do People Become Librarians?

People go to college to become librarians.

They learn to help people choose books.

Librarians are people who love books.

Quiz

Can you remember what these things are called?

Look for the answers on page 24.

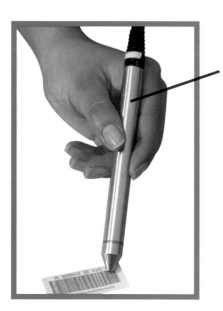 **?**

 **?**

Picture Glossary

bookmobile
page 14

reference books
page 18

businesspeople
page 15

scanning wand
page 8

computer
pages 5, 8

Note to Parents and Teachers

Reading for information is an important part of a child's literacy development. Learning begins with a question about something. Help children think of themselves as investigators and researchers by encouraging their questions about the world around them. Each chapter in this book begins with a question. Read the question together. Look at the pictures. Talk about what you think the answer might be. Then read the text to find out if your predictions were correct. Think of other questions you could ask about the topic, and discuss where you might find the answers. Assist children in using the picture glossary and the index to practice new vocabulary and research skills.

Index

Answers to quiz on page 22

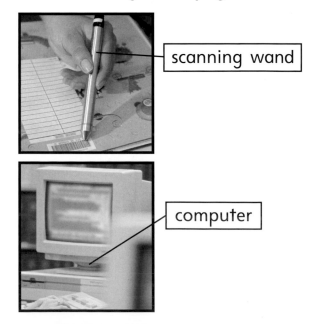

scanning wand

computer